Buried Treasures

by

Al Lauer

DORRANCE PUBLISHING CO., INC.
PITTSBURGH, PENNSYLVANIA 15222

ISBN: 978-0-8059-7753-0

Printed in the United States of America

First Printing

For more information or to order additional books, please contact:
Dorrance Publishing Co., Inc.
701 Smithfield Street
Third Floor
Pittsburgh, Pennsylvania 15222
U.S.A.
1-800-788-7654
www.dorrancebookstore.com

Dedicated to all those who stuck by me and maintained their belief in me during the difficult times.

Contents

Section One:
Spirituality

A Buried Treasure

On a day quite dark and dreary—causing mind and soul to weary—
I sat beside the fire quite contented with myself.
I entertained the thought of dozing, and my eyes were ever-closing,
focused, vaguely, on a bookcase and the books upon the shelf.

Yes, books of many volumes forming multi-colored columns
awed my imagination in the secrets they must hold.
My aimless fingers wandered as through these books I pondered.
Then, by chance, I found one volume that was ragged, torn, and old.

I thought best it be discarded, for the price of time had marred it,
and it bore a musty odor caused by ever-growing mold,
but I happened to discover 'neath the dust upon its cover
the inscription, "Holy Bible," lettered now in faded gold.

So, I probed amongst its pages with its history of the ages,
at first with passing interest, then transformed to utter awe,
the story of creation with its wealth of information
to the sheer appreciation of God's wondrous, perfect law.

I then read how shepherds trembled when angelic forms assembled
to bring forth the joyous message of a wondrous virgin birth.
Within sin-infested nations, there was need of God's salvation,
so our Lord, with love and mercy, placed His Son upon the earth.

It told how Peter thrice denied Him. In result, they crucified Him.
Jesus murmured, "It is finished," with His last and dying breath.
His body was imprisoned. Three days later, He was risen
and His mission, thus completed—even victory over death.

I then lay the book beside me, analyzed the thoughts inside me,
and I marveled at the message that this great book had to tell.

Within its beaten cover was a "treasure" to discover—
rich in paradise eternal and escape from Satan's hell.

Now I cannot help but wonder of this world so torn asunder,
in which greed will form a ladder by which man can raise himself.
Man will go about his labor, cheating brother, friend, and neighbor,
while, unopened, lies a Bible, gathering dust upon a shelf.

I can draw but one conclusion why we're plagued with such confusion,
My philosophy is simple, although, some might think it odd.
In man's constant search for pleasure, he's misplaced a priceless
treasure—
a guide for life—for love and happiness by the greatest author—
God!

My Prayer

I pray Thee, Lord, who's up above,
whose word is peace, whose power is love,
to guide us through these troubled times,
and through our lives, may your light shine.

I ask Thee, Lord, that I may be
a constant witness of service to Thee.
I ask for strength for this new day,
that I might show someone the way.

I ask Thee, Lord, if it's Thy will,
this war to end—these guns to still
so many soldiers dying alone,
so many families crying at home.

Lord, war is hell—the grief is great,
feelings of torment, feelings of hate.
I know that before this day is through
many will die without knowing You.

I ask for Thy guidance for this war to cease.
I ask that Thou show us the true way to peace.
Oh, Lord, if Thou wills it, I pray that we be
one nation united in worshipping Thee.

Forgive us our sins, Lord—it's us who's to blame.
These things I ask for in Jesus Christ's name, amen!

Look at Our World

Look at our world—a peaceful place.
Look at the children with smiling face.
Look at this memory, now in the past.
Look at the peace—why didn't it last?
Look at the mother, tears in her eyes.
Look at the child in innocence cry.
Look at a war—death fills the sky.
Look at their grief—their soldier has died.
Look at our world—the oceans still roar.
Look at our world at peace no more.

Oh, Lord up above,
send us mercy—send us love,
take our grief—take our pain,
make our world at peace again.

Look at the rose—its petals still bright.
Look at the bird still winging its flight.
Look at the river—still flows to the sea.
Look at these thoughts that no longer can be.
Look at the rose—its petals have died.
Look at the bird with nowhere to fly.
Look at the river, now stained with blood.
Look at our world in absence of love.

Oh, Lord up above,
send us mercy—send us love,
take our grief—take our pain,
make our world at peace again.

Look at our world, now torn apart.
Look at the grief that has entered the heart.

Look at the sin that rules over all.
Look at the man who no longer stands tall.
Look at the child who cries out in fear.
Look at the greed we cherish so dear.
Look at our world—its contents of shame.
Look now on us, who are to blame.

Oh, Lord up above,
send us mercy—send us love,
take our grief—take our pain,
make our world at peace again.

Somewhere

Somewhere there must be a solution
to the hatred and pollution
in this swirling sphere we call our "Mother Earth."
Somewhere there must be fellowship
with friendship and companionship,
where our judgment is the value of our mirth.

Somewhere there must be flowers.
You could pass away the hours,
watch the sunset form God's painting in the sky
Somewhere, there must be gentleness,
Tranquility, and tenderness,
where your visions just bring beauty to your eyes.

Somewhere there is paradise
without poverty or sacrifice.
Golden paths replace the earthen sod.
Somewhere there's eternity,
sincerity, tranquility.
Somewhere I will finally meet my God.

Lonely Little Chapel

I was traveling all alone one Sunday morning
through a little town not very far from home.
All the faces that I saw were those of strangers,
but they smiled with a joy I've never known.

I walked a narrow path, so long and winding,
and a chapel with a cross came into view.
I heard the voices of the congregation singing
hymns of praises, songs of love and life anew.

Yes, a simple, hidden, lonely, little chapel
with a steeple reaching to the skies above,
Filled with music and the sound of happy people
praising Jesus and His everlasting love.

So, I walked into that lonely, little chapel.
A stained glass window was the first to catch my eye,
the image of our Lord and precious Savior
kneeling down with His face raised to the sky.

Although He knew that He was soon to be imprisoned,
Although He knew that He'd be crucified to die,
He knew He must do His Father's business,
and now He lives for the sake of you and I.

Yes, a simple, hidden, lonely, little chapel
With a steeple reaching to the skies above,
filled with music and the sound of happy people,
praising Jesus, and His everlasting love.

Dedicated to Pastor Kyle Key and all my friends at Roxborough
Presbyterian Church

Jesus

Jesus, you're my rock, my foundation,
you're my king, you're my Lord,
you're the one I'll adore ever more.

Jesus, you're my strength, my salvation,
fill my heart, fill my soul,
take my sin, make me whole and secure.

You're my teacher, my holy redeemer,
you're my comfort, my savior and king.

Jesus, you're the gift from the Father.
Spread your arms open wide.
In your love, I'll abide evermore.

Mary

Mary, who is this child that you bear?
Are you aware of the cross He'll have to bear
for people everywhere?

Mary, who is this son that you bore?
Will He be loved and adored
forever more?

Will these miracles that he performs
lead him to a crown of thorns,
this child of yours, this child of yours?

Mary, bow down your head, wipe your eyes.
Your son is crucified. Do you know why
He has to die?

Do you know? Is He our Lord?
Will He live on forever more,
this child of yours, this child of yours?

Mary, lift up your head, Dry your eyes.
Your son is alive. He did arise,
and you know He is our Lord.
He'll live on forever more,
this child of yours, this child of yours.

Put Him First

My Savior died for me upon the cross of Calvary.
He shed His blood for me to bear my sins and set me free.

Jesus, my savior, Jesus, my king,
put Him first within your life.
Put Him first ahead of everything.

My savior promised then He would rise and live again.
He lives within my soul, and now my life's in His control.

Jesus, my Savior, Jesus, my king,
put Him first within your life.
Put Him first ahead of everything.

My savior welcomes you. Give Him your life and live anew.
He's with you everyday. He's just a simple prayer away.

Jesus, my savior, Jesus, my king,
put Him first within your life.
Put Him first ahead of everything.

A Path of Deliverance

I often think of the years before
and the many things that I adored.
A little boy with curious eyes,
I'd watch the birds as they flew by.
I marveled at their ease of flight
and how they disappeared at night.
They'd roost and sleep the night away,
but, with the sun, another day.
The "sun," another wondrous sight,
how, in the morn , it gives its light.
Its brightness, growing, you wonder how.
Its heat and warmth, you feel it now.
And, with its rise, it seems to say,
"Sleepy eyes, wake up. It's now a new day."
This fire-filled giant, with light so bright,
what a shame it must give way to night.
My thoughts now change to other things,
to crawling creatures that come with spring.
I'd watch a snake behind a glass.
With interest keen, the hours would pass.
With Army life, the guns would roar.
I'd live with death within a war.
I'd pray to God, who's up above,
"Lord, end this war. Restore the love."
I wonder if God plans the fate,
to end this world so filled with hate.
It's foolish for one war to end
and have another start again.
It seems so senseless in my eyes,
why war lives on and peace will die.
Is it power that will make men strive
to cause a war and loss of lives?

But, power is the seed of hate.
Is it worth serving Satan's fate?
The fate of war sometimes is strange.
Through a war, a man's life will change.
A soldier, on guard, may be standing alone.
His mind often wanders to his family back home.
Then, suddenly, combat—"death" everywhere.
He cries out to the Lord above,
that invisible being with merciful love,
so based on confusion, inspired by fears,
His prayer is uttered, and our Lord Jesus hears.
The soldier then realizes he's not alone,
For he felt his deliverance, and God's glory is shown,
and now, as a Christian, his story, he'll tell,
"I found my Lord Jesus through the terrors of hell."
I still have my interests, just like before,
but now, in my heart, it's the Lord, I adore.
I now look at nature and the message it brings,
"In the beginning, God created these things!"

Section Two:
Love, Lost and Found

I'll Remember You

I'll remember how we met and won't forget—
the ease of our first meeting.
I'll remember your easy style—your ready smile—
the warmness of your greeting.

I'll remember all the jokes said of other folks—
the foolish lives they're living.
I'll remember your "wondering" eyes—that look of surprise—
for a birthday gift, once given.

Yes, I'll remember our times together.
They will live forever in my mind.
They will live forever in my heart and in my soul,
and the memories will be of beautiful things,
For my time with you was truly beautiful.

I'll remember your ways.
I'll remember all the ways you spoke in praise
to share my company.
I'll remember your caress—your tenderness—
during times of privacy.
I'll remember a week, once shared—the sun in your hair—
the hours we spent together.
I'll remember holding your hand—playing in sand—
how we wished it could last forever.

Yes, I'll always remember you,
for, in you, I have learned a new happiness—
a warmth I've never known before.
In you, I have a memory of something beautiful,
something real, and something pure.

I'll remember you as the years pass,
and the memories will last,
filled with happiness and thankfulness to you.
In you, I have a memory that's unblemished,
not to be diminished with time.
In you, I have finally met love,
and time cannot deny it once was mine.

I Really Loved You after All

I can't forget the times we shared—those August nights—
the sandy beach—the salty air. I'd hold you tight—
the crazy times—those funny names—
without you, nothing's quite the same,
and I guess I really loved you after all

Now that we've gone our separate ways, I think of you.
I wonder how you spend your days. That's all I do.
There must be reason for this pain.
I wish that things were right again,
and I guess I really loved you after all

Now I find myself wanting to see you—
still wishing to hold you so near—
and I'm hoping you still think about me.
It's so hard holding back all these tears

A word of thanks before I'm through. I must confess,
those special times I shared with you were happiness.
Yes, I regret what might have been.
I'd gladly do it all again,
and I guess I really loved you after all

Though another may hold and possess you
and may whisper his words tenderly,
I just hope that the love that he gives you
is as pure as the love you gave me.

I must go on, must live my life, put on a smile.
It's just a mask I'll have to wear a little while.
These are the things I have to do,
but all I do is think of you,
and I guess I really love you after all.

Special Lady

Have I changed you, special lady? Was it my suspicious mind?
Did I speak of love too early? Were the words I used unkind?

Are you troubled, special lady? Can I lend a helping hand?
Can this pain I feel be buried? Will I ever understand?

Special lady, lovely lady,
You were always so special to me.
Now you're going, and I'm showing
that sadness is my specialty.

Are you leaving, special lady? Is there time to say "goodbye"?
Will you leave me sad and lonely? Will I always wonder why?

Won't I see you, special lady? Don't you want me for a friend?
Has your fire turned to ashes? Has our time come to an end?

Special lady, lovely lady,
You were always so special to me.
Now you're going and I'm showing
that sadness is my specialty.

If it's over, special lady, I can't change the way you feel,
but I'll thank you, and I'll miss you, and I'll know our time was real.
I will kiss you, pretty baby, just a tearful kiss goodbye,
but you'll be my special lady until the day I die.

Special lady, lovely lady,
you were always so special to me.
Now you're going, and I'm showing
that sadness is my specialty.

To a Natural Beauty

If ever I was asked to describe you,
I would liken you to all that is beautiful,

like the soft, fragile beauty of a rose.
Such is your softness, and through this softness
your beauty is thus magnified.

If ever I was asked to describe you,
I would liken you to an evening sunset
with its colors blending,
painting nature's portrait in a golden sky.

Such would be your portrait,
for, like a sunset, your beauty is magnetic,
drawing attention to itself,
holding one's eyes with its inner-magnificence
that cannot help but shine outwardly.

Your beauty is natural,
not attained by artificial means.

Your beauty shines through your eyes.
It is heard in your voice.
It is felt in your gentle smile and touch,
and to know you is to know "pure" beauty itself.

I Love You Too Much to Be Friends

You take my hand and wish me well.
Now I suffer in my private hell.
Just sitting home—right by the phone—
but I won't call.

Your tone has changed. Your eyes are cold.
I guess somehow I'm being told,
with nothing said, the flame is dead—
no love at all.

It's for the best that I departed—
Not a word, just let it all end.
I'd rather not see you and be broken-hearted.
I love you too much to be friends.

No one to see, nowhere to go,
I just listen to the radio,
but then a song of love gone wrong,
I think of you.

The music falls upon my ears.
There's just no holding back the tears.
Turn off the light. Call it a night
for being blue.

It's for the best that I departed—
not a word, just let it all end.
I'd rather not see you and be broken-hearted.
I love you too much to be friends.

I walk the streets we used to walk,
remembering how we used to talk—

your little grin. What could've been
will never be.

Two lovers pass. She holds him tight,
the way we were on other nights.
I start to cry and turn my eyes
so they won't see.

It's for the best that I departed—
not a word, just let it all end.
I'd rather not see you and be broken-hearted.
I love you too much to be friends.

Someday I might just take a chance
and fall into a new romance.
I don't know when I'll love again,
a love that's true.

I see the girls with loving eyes.
I leave them to the other guys
'cause, don't you see, there'll never be
another you.

It's for the best that I departed—
not a word, just let it all end.
I'd rather not see you and be broken-hearted.
I love you too much to be friends.

I Remember Summer

I remember summer.
I remember warm and sunny skies, your laughing, cheerful eyes,
taking sips of wine, laughing all the time.

I remember summer.
I remember salty ocean air, the sunlight in your hair,
walking hand in hand, playing in the sand.

But, now summer's over, and it's over with you.
The summer left and left me feeling blue.

I remember summer.
I remember walks along the shore, a shell you just adored,
our bodies, cold and numb, waiting for the sun.

I remember summer.
I remember hikes within the park, kissing in the dark,
looking in your eyes, warm and tender sighs.

But, now summer's over, and it's over with you.
The summer left and left me feeling blue.

I remember summer.
I remember warming to your smile, your bright and cheerful style,
expressions on your face, a meaningful embrace.
I remember resting in your arms, sharing all your charms,
feeling your caress, times of tenderness,
warming to your touch, wanting you so much,
holding you so tight, loving you at night.

Yes, I'll remember summer, and I'll remember you,
but the summer left and left me feeling blue.

One More Time Around

Yes, it was over. We had gone our separate ways—
such a shame—no one to blame—just one of those days.

People tell me,
"Love will come around when you least expect it!"
"Just like it did before!"
"It will lift you up, so brighten up!"
I said, "No! No more!"

I thought, "It couldn't happen!"
"No! No more next times!"
I'm looking at my past. The passion never lasts
for a long time.
"No! No more next times!"

Then, someone told me,
"Love is never gone! Someone will come along!
"You've got that light inside you!"
"Someone will turn it on!"

I don't want to do it,
go for one more time around.
No! Not after the last time.
That was the "Last" time.
There's still too much inside me,
and this mask I wear can't hide me.
A real love is hard to find—any kind!

But, maybe—maybe one more time—
What might I find?
Life is full of gives and takes,
and I know I made mistakes,

but I must try to get it right,
put my sorrow out of sight,
get back to life—stop being down—
just one more time around!

Second-Hand Fool

You meet a girl, and you believe
that you could never be deceived—
not you—a guy who knows the score
through experiences years before,
but, yet, though foolishly, you know
you let your true emotions grow,
though, still, you hide your feelings deep
inside of you and try to keep
the secret of your hasty heart
that recently began to start
to beat more rapidly, it seems
reliving again once broken dreams.
But, maybe she's the one for you,
and maybe now your search is through.

So, you introduce her to your friend,
knowing not that it would end
with you so quickly, bowing out
for the guy she cared the "least" about.

Now again, you must defend your pride—
though secretly you know you've cried,
but, to them, you laugh and play it cool,
and you wonder how you could be the fool
to let yourself be hurt again
by the girl you love and the guy, your "friend"!

Now again, you keep yourself confined
to solitude of heart and mind,
and, again, you build that lonely wall
to protect you lest again you fall,
for you fear that, if you fall again,

it means that you'll be hurt again,
a hurt that you can't bear again,
so, thus, you stay alone!

Reunion

Thirty plus years have passed
much too quickly, I'm afraid.
When a chance reunion developed—
maybe—was it a chance?
Was it meant to be?
Possibly, yes.
Was it an accident?
Who knows? Who cares?
I'm just grateful for the experience
of just seeing you again.

Reliving the memories of an earlier time—
time that, somehow, stayed vivid in our minds,
memories that never diminished or eroded
with the passing of the years.

Our time was an innocent time—
an emotional time—
a time when the feelings were real.
The feelings were pure and unrestricted
in their depth.

It was the first real emotion of that kind
for us both—an attraction, a magnetism,
and, yes, a "first love"—
containing all the aspects of what love contains—
joy, laughter, hurt, pain,
passion, tears, comfort, communication,
highs, lows, sharing, caring,
hugs, kisses, misunderstandings,
and long-lasting gazes between tear-filled eyes.

"Unchained Melody," that was the catalyst
to set forces of emotion into motion.

To see you again is a treasure.
It's amazing how the chemistry
is still in abundance—
yes—even after all these years

Lives have changed.
Our separate paths took us in different directions.
We've experienced different things—
good and bad, happy and sad—

but, regardless where
our separate lives may take us,
I know now, after this reunion,
after all these thirty-plus years,
that you, Carol, will always
be my "Gidget,"
and I will always be
your "Soldier Boy,"
and yes—even after all these years—
like it or not, the love is still there.

Dedicated to Carol

What Keeps a Friendship Alive

What keeps a friendship alive?

Maybe it's just anticipating a warm smile, knowing all the while
it will be there as anticipated.
Maybe, it's in the lives that we share—the problems we must bear—
and never to feel obligated.

What keeps a friendship alive?

That, in times both good and bad, both of us are glad
to share our lives and communion.
And, in times when we're apart, deep within our hearts,
we can enjoy our separate union.

What keeps a friendship alive?

During times filled with sorrow, there's a brighter tomorrow.
We both have someone who cares.
And, with life's ebb and flow, we have somewhere to go
for a shoulder that's strong to bear.

What keeps a friendship alive?

To keep understanding when you're not understanding—
giving love when it's not asked of you.
And when others turn away, you have the words to say,
and you do the things you have to do.
You are asking without prying—advising without lying.
To give solace, you always strive.
Love, understanding, never demanding—
that keeps a friendship alive!

Dedicated to "Margaret," my closest and dearest friend

Section Three:
War

A Letter to Parents

A child is born in warmth and grace.
Two parents gaze upon his face,
in their eyes, a priceless gem,
this new creation, a part of them.
Their child—a boy with curly hair,
they raise him with the best of care.
And now, at school, two parents wait
to see their young son graduate.
You've raised him well, so take your bow,
but Uncle Sam, he wants him now.
So, with induction, worry starts.
They bid goodbye with troubled hearts.
Yes, worry, masked behind a grin.
They pray, "Dear Lord, take care of him."
He breaks the news of Vietnam.
"I'll be okay. Don't worry, Mom."
Aboard a ship with gun in hand,
he journeys to this far-off land,
a land of strife, a land of war.
Their son is not a child anymore.
Yes, in this land, so ripped and torn,
a child has died. A man is born.

The Law of Survival

The soldier sleeps upon nightfall,
but then at dawn, the wake-up call—
a broken dream and weary eyes—
his "friend," a gun, beside him lies.
To the east, a rising sun
greeted by a firing gun.
He checks his water, then his pack.
His home is strapped upon his back—
his water, his power, his senses, his guide.
His camouflaged enemy will always hide.
Perspiring freely—unmerciful heat—
he'll trod the jungle with burning feet.
Through this steaming, jungle home,
his enemy roams!

With a stalking silence, with a deathly hush,
he spies a movement in the brush.
Then, suddenly a burst. Death fills the air.
He looks at his prey with a heart of despair,
what once was a man, he is no more.
A bullet-torn body, a hideous gore.
A family man? Well, who can tell—
a face of stone, a fate of hell.
The soldier, then, must look away,
ignore his crime, the price he'll pay.

The sun is high. He's soaking wet.
That bullet-torn body he will never forget.
He stalks again with hidden pain,
but he knows that he must kill again.
The soldier does not pride his kill.
The law of survival says he will.

Then, finally a clearing, another camp.
The sun is down. The air is damp.
The soldier, again asleep, he'll lie.
His future—face another day!

Time Passes On

A girl and a boy, their hearts filled with joy,
their feelings were the same.
With their vows being said, they were just wed.
Now she was wearing his name.
A letter arrived that would change both their lives,
turn their whole world upside-down.
He looked in her eyes as she started to cry,
and he tried to calm her down.
He wiped tears from her face as they gently embraced,
kissed her lips, and held her head.
She continued to cry, kept asking, "Why?"
So, finally he said,

"Oh, baby, don't you cry now.
No, we're not saying 'Goodbye,' now.
It won't be too long, and time passes on."

His orders arrived—no big surprise.
He would ship across the sea.
He'd soon be in a war, a fact he can't ignore.
This was how it had to be.
He said, "It won't be long. Promise me you'll be strong,"
still holding her embrace.
"I may be far away, but I'll write you everyday,"
but the tears streamed down her face.

"Oh, baby, don't you cry now.
No, we're not saying, 'Goodbye' now.
It won't be too long, and time passes on."

He was writing a letter, saying things would be better.
An explosion, an orange-red glare—

they were under attack, and the soldiers fought back,
each saying his own silent prayer.
The fighting was bad, and the outcome was sad.
Many souls were lost in the fight.
A boy they found in the mud, face down,
with these words clenched in his hand tight,

"Oh, baby, don't you cry now.
No, we're not saying, 'Goodbye' now.
It won't be too long, and time passes on."

Dedication to an Amputee

He just got out of high school. He was athletic,
played all the sports, got good reports.
It's so pathetic.

Still loved his first girlfriend—they just got married.
She was his girl—she was his world.
Her pictures, he carried.

He was forced into duty, those army orders.
Vietnam going strong, it wouldn't be long—
he would soon leave our borders.

He was put into combat—the 9th division.
Just like us all, his number was called—
not our decision.

He went out on a mission—the rainy season—
With the Mekong in flood, we were bogged down in mud—
no rhyme or reason.

That's when it happened, that foul situation—
the trucks being loaded, a grenade exploded.
He would need amputation.

Epilogue

The surgery's long over. Both legs were severed.
He is my friend now 'til the end,
now and forever.

A real horror story—a sad situation—
we talk for awhile. He still wears a smile.
He's my inspiration.

So, now in conclusion to this sorrow-filled letter,
his marriage stayed strong as the years rolled along.
"Life couldn't be better."

Dedicated to Donny, Vietnam, 1967.

A Quiet Hero

He was just another soldier, a face in the crowd.
He wasn't outspoken. He didn't talk loud.
He told no one his troubles, his hardships, or cares.
He never said much—just a word here and there.
He liked to get letters from his mom and his dad.
He liked to think back to the good times he had.
He looked forward to the day when his family he'd see.
He often imagined just how it would be.
He was never considered courageous or bold.
He just followed his orders and did what was told.
He was just another soldier—nothing more.
He had no bright medals for heroics in war.
He never made headlines, never noted for fame.
I doubt if you knew him by face or by name.
When told of his death, sure, his parents, they cried,
but most didn't know who this boy was who died.
His memory will last for us soldiers who live.
He's a "Quiet Hero." He gave all he could give!

Dedicated to William Thompson—Vietnam 1967

Fiasco
Vietnam 1967

Just a lot of "whys," a lot of questions
with undefined answers,
a lot of the inevitable ironies of war
without ever being classified as a "war,"
a recipe for the concoction of the poison
given the cutesy name "conflict"
or maybe "police action"
rather than calling it what it really is—"War."

But, the powers that be
really can't call it "war."
That word is far too brutal a word
to be used in their public conversation.

But, does it really matter
what word is used to describe Vietnam?
Is there a word that is sufficient?
An efficient word to adequately portray
the horrors of this day,
where families bow and pray
the loss of lives we all endured.
Is this our "patriotic mission,"
or have we lapsed into submission?
Can we be so self-assured?
Is there a word, a catch-all phrase?
"Patriotic duty," a "free democracy"?
Is it "peace with honor" or total "lunacy"?
Will there ever be a winner?
Are we the saints and they the sinner?
Will there ever be conclusion? Is this war or just illusion?
Can't we stop all this confusion?
Let's just bring our soldiers home!

Section Four:

Variety

Utopian Discovery

When I was younger, in my prime,
I used to daydream to pass the time
of tropic isles—distant lands—
with bending palms and sun-bleached sands,
of island girls with long, black hair,
of flowery fields to scent the air,
of tropic sunsets, colors bright,
precluding diamond stars of night.
Gentle waves kiss the coral beach,
volcanic peaks, the clouds to reach.
All these were imagined scenes,
but this I found in the Philippines.
This land once was a battleground,
but now a paradise I found.
Memories of war one can't erase,
but the people wear a smiling face.
They're generous, kind, eager to please—
a land to grace the Pacific seas.
The long-haired girl with sparkling eye,
her beauty, no one can deny.
With mountains, lakes, and other sights,
to cities with their glowing lights,
these once were imagined dreams.
A "dream come true," the Philippines!

Depression

What is depression? A sad expression,
feelings of gloom, locked in your room,
hopeless oppression.

Cut off from all others—fathers and mothers—
relationships end—neighbors and friends,
sisters and brothers.

Try medication, seeking elation,
taking a pill, hoping it will
bring reparation.

Those who are caring seem overbearing.
You resist their embrace, slam the door in their face—
no mood for sharing.

No point in bathing, no point in shaving.
No one to see. That's how it must be—
the way you're behaving.

Pure isolation of endless duration—
last night, you cried, thought suicide—
life's termination.

Some call it affliction. Some say it's just fiction.
The truth is you're ill with no power to still
your sadness addiction.

As I write this letter, thank God, I'm much better.
Through those who have cared, through the power of prayer,
my life's now together!

Death is Mine

"DEATH!"
A mere five letter word that brings fear
to the minds of young and old alike.

"DEATH!"
Just an image of void—a sea of doom—
knowing not when it will strike.

Oh, holy and eternal "DEATH!"
Why are you to be feared
when you're thought to be near?
Why are you scorned and not adorned
by those you claimed for your own?
Can it be that our greed
for this life that we lead
Only ends when we face you alone?

Oh, mysterious, most powerful "DEATH!"
Are we a blinded mess of loneliness
to attempt to flee thy sword?
Can it be that your sting is the song that you sing,
and your tomb is our just reward?

Alas, oh noble "DEATH,"
perhaps it's you that I crave with your eternal grave,
and perhaps your peace is divine.
For at life I have lost.
Lo, when our paths are crossed,
at last, oh, "DEATH," you'll be mine!

Tribute to a Real Man

We were just kids, just in our teens.
We were no angels by any means.
Hanging on corners to pass the time.
Youthful endeavors, mischievous minds.
As usual, we gathered on summer nights,
laughing and joking, sometimes getting in fights.
Out of the darkness, a stranger appeared.
We grew silent and watched him as he slowly neared.
He approached us and stopped, a smile on his face.
This first memory of him will be never erased.
We were just kids. He was older than us.
Not many older ones teenagers trust,
but he had a most disarming way,
and, with a smile, he began to say,
"Hey, guys, can you help me? I sure need a hand!"
"My name is Harold!" and then he shook hands.
He said he's the pastor of the church up the street.
A friendlier guy you will never meet.
"We're forming a ball team!" he continued to say,
"We don't have many people who are able to play!
We need ballplayers! Can you help us out?"
Then he told us what the league was about.
We would play other teams—schedules and all—
umpires on hand to make the calls.
This all sounded good, but, he continued to say,
there's one rule we must follow in order to play.
"Our church has one rule that you cannot bend."
"Two Sundays a month, you must attend."
We never played in a league. This was all new.
Two Sundays a month, we filled up the back pew.
Harold showed interest, took me under his wing,
answered my questions about anything,

45

took me off of the corners, introduced me to God.
I found God through baseball—sounds kind of odd—
all through this pastor and his smiling face,
all through the love of his God he embraced.
His death was so sudden, so premature.
Just in his forties, his heart failed to endure.
He's now with his savior. He's at home at last.
His life was well-lived. His imprint was cast.
He was my mentor, my idol, my friend.
Someday, in God's glory, I'll see him again.

Dedicated in memory of Pastor Harold R. Mulvaney

A Double

Funny thing happened the other day.
I'm on the street, just going my way.
There's a voice behind me saying, "Hi, Ed!"
I pause, I stop, I turn my head.
He says, "Hi, Ed, How have you been?"
I know I've never laid eyes on him.
I said, "I'm sorry, I'm not him!"
He wrinkled his brow and rubbed his chin
"You look just like my doctor. That's really funny!"
I replied, "Well, I wish I had his Money!"
He said, "Really! You have a Double!"
I said, "I sure hope he stays out of trouble!"
"Well, nice meeting you," I started to say.
He still looked confused as he turned away.
Then he stopped again, turning his head.
"Are you sure your name isn't Ed?"
I replied, "I think I ought to know my name!"
He answered, "You two look the same!"
Then we went our separate ways.
Maybe I'll meet "Doctor Ed" someday!

Opposites

They're sisters. It's hard to believe.
From the same parents, they were conceived.
The younger was blond, blue-eyed, and fair.
The older with dark eyes, matching her hair.

The younger was vainer, applying her make-up—
many dates, many boyfriends, many breakups.
The older was plainer, more into studies.
Not many people she could call buddies.

The younger went out often, dancing and skating.
The older was home-bound, not into dating.
One was outgoing, a gleam to her eye.
One was secretive, kept emotions inside.

The younger had street-smarts, nobody's fool.
The older had intellect, more into school.
Yes, they are sisters—hard to believe.
From the same parents, they were conceived.

The Hunter

"It is Ravenous."
Its hunger unfulfilled, it must hunt its prey.
Its craving must be filled this very day.
"It is the Hunter."

Searching out the site, it must set its pace.
Needs must be met tonight, go to the place.
"It is Approaching."

Nearing to its goal, its eyes are fixated.
Separate one from the whole, its senses elated.
"It has Selected."

Singled out the unsuspecting, the one to fill its need,
success it is expecting. The one on which to feed.
"It is Preparing."

Inching forward to get close—stealth, anticipation—
this one it wants the most. Successful expectation.
"It's now Attacking."

It needs to be fed. Now is the time.
It raises its head and says, "Hi, What's your sign?"

Fishing with Dad

I loved fishing, always loved fishing.
"Let's go out to the bay!"
"Such a nice day!"
This is what I was wishing.

Dad had a boat, a little boat.
I patiently waited
as Dad hesitated.
Then, finally, he reached for his coat.

Now we're out on the water, choppy water.
We then baited our lines.
Everything's fine—
just what the doctor ordered.

The fish were biting, really biting.
The flounder just waited
for our hooks to be baited.
I was happy and excited.

Dad started the engine. Why start the engine?
"Let's move over there!"
I asked, "Over where?
They're biting here!" I started to mention.

We changed our location, a new location.
Now nothing is biting,
our bait not inviting.
The fish went on vacation!

We moved different places, many new places.
Every half hour,

he'd turn on the power.
Then it's off to the races!

Dad saw my expression. He started confessin'.
He said, "When we're still,
"I start feeling ill."
To me, this made an impression!

"Let's try trolling. We move if we're trolling."
We trolled our way in,
boring as sin.
Next time, we'll go bowling!

We Watched Our Mom

We watched our mom—
Loving, giving,
a life so rich in its living.
Laughing, caring,
constantly loving and sharing.
Thinking of others,
a beautiful, unselfish mother.
Held us together.
She'd talk and we would feel better.

We watched our mom—
Stricken, paralyzed,
thoroughly tested and analyzed.
Doctors being careful.
Mom remained hopeful and prayerful.
Praying, talking,
hoping, someday, she'd be walking.
Her body losing feeling,
no sign of a cure or of healing.

We watched our mom—
Laughing, kidding.
Now in a wheelchair, she's sitting.
Resigned to her condition.
To be loving was her only mission.
In bed, laying,
earnestly, sincerely praying.
Talking to her Savior,
this was her honest behavior.

We watched our mom—
Peaceful, dying.

All of the family was crying.
Now they're together.
She'll dwell with her savior forever!

Dedicated to our mom—"the center of the family"

Someone You Didn't Like

Did you ever meet someone you didn't like?
You know what I'm talking about.
You know without a doubt—
someone that you never want to see again ever,
someone you can live without!

Someone that you just can't stand—
doesn't matter, woman or man
or that kid who's so spoiled, it makes your blood boil.
You want to give him the back of your hand!

There's a neighbor who lives on my street.
Never fails, we always meet.
He will talk me to death with his horrible breath—
almost knocks me right off of my feet!

There's the one who gives you a frown.
On their luck, they're so very down.
So, you lend them some money. Isn't it funny?
Now they're nowhere to be found!

I was driving on my vacation,
a cop, in the bushes, just waitin'.
He gave me a ticket—almost told him to "stick it."
Fifty dollars worth of frustration!

The boss who turned down your promotion,
after giving him years of devotion.
You could wring his neck. You're a nervous wreck—
a lot of nervous emotion!

Then, there are ones with that certain style—

a great big toothy-white smile.
They come over and hug you. This really bugs you.
They're stabbing at your back all the while!

It seems like they're all around us.
"Good grief, they're gonna surround us—
the bozo's, the clowner's, the uppers, the downers."
They all overwhelm and abound us!

You must listen to their chatter.
If you don't, it doesn't matter.
"His face is too boney. Her breasts are so phony."
You feel like climbing a ladder!

There are those who love to lecture
their opinions beyond conjecture.
Any subject at all, they're an expert on all.
You'd like to give them an obscene gesture!

You got a lawyer to handle your brief.
He'll represent you—what a relief.
Then he hands you his bill, and you're suddenly ill.
This guy is a legal thief!

Even our Lord felt the passion—
went into the temple whip-lashin',
and this is no fable. He kicked over tables
and gave them all a good tongue-lashin'!

He went on a mountain to preach
a subject He wanted to teach.
"You must love these people, too. Not just the ones loving you."

But, Lord, that's not easy to love someone "sleazy."
What in the world can I do?

We must pause and count to ten.
Still no good? Do it over again!
Did your blood pressure rise? Turn your head to the skies,
and say "Lord, be with me. Amen!"

Hammered

He was hammered!
Drunk, out of his mind again.
Gone into town, making his rounds,
staggering, stumbling,
not thinking, just drinking again.

Totally hammered—
drank himself blind again
with his blood-shot eyes and D.U.I.s,
awaking, escaping again.

Yes, he was hammered,
Stammering, stupor again.
When did he start falling apart,
his life unwinding, quickly declining?
When will this tragedy end?

Denial

I see her as she passes again, wearing those sunglasses.
I know it's just to hide her blackened eyes.
A new bruise is on her arm. I'm not really that alarmed.
She's been hit again. I'm not really that surprised.

Many times before, the cops have been called to her door.
The neighbors could hear the loud commotion.
Sometimes they'd take him in—next day, he's back again.
The same pattern is again set into motion.

Asked why she doesn't leave him.
"He says he's sorry. I believe him.
Sometimes he reacts without really thinking.
He'll then start pushin' and shovin',
But, deep inside, I really love him,
and he only hurts me after he's been drinking."

She continues her excuses for enduring her abuses.
She says he is the father of her kids.
"I want to stay together. Things will get a whole lot better.
He will change." So far, he never did.

Yes, I see her as she passes, still wearing those sunglasses.
I just shake my head and have to wonder why.
People living in denial, their lives a downward spiral,
but, for the grace of God, walk you or I.

I'm Gonna Be a Daddy

Well, it's gonna happen. I'm gonna be a Daddy!

Me, a guy who's thirty-eight, kinda straight,
hair turning gray—seems funny to say—"I'm gonna be a Daddy!"

Yep, it's gonna happen. I'm gonna be a Daddy!
And, my lady is the mommy!
And, what do you know, she's starting to show,
getting a tummy. Seems kinda funny—
her, wearing those jeans, too tight, it seems,
and it seems funny to say, "I'm gonna be a Daddy!"

Maybe a little girl, all snuggled in a pink blanket
with her wondering eyes and a look of surprise
at this vast, new world to explore,
and "Who's that grown-up standing there?
Yeah, him, the one with the gray in his hair!"
"That's me, your Daddy!"

Watching her with her first doll,
saying her first words,
taking her first steps,
wearing her first pony-tail,
my little angel, and I'm her Daddy!

But, then again, what if it's a boy?
Well, that means bunk-beds, baseball, football,
Spiderman, Batman, Superman, and, oh yes,
his cousin's hand-me-down clothes and toys.

But—what a joy—a boy

to ask all the questions in the world about—
frogs and toads, football, baseball, baby brother,
and, someday, he'll ask about girls!
That's when mommy says, "Go ask your Father!"

Me? A father?

How do you change a diaper?
How do you make formula?
Do you hold your nose when the baby makes a mess?
I can't even handle it when the dog makes a mess!

But, yes, I'm gonna be a Daddy!
And we got to get ready. My lady's craving spaghetti!
So, if you see me smile in just a little while,
"I'm gonna be a Daddy!"

'Twas the Week before Christmas

'Twas the week before Christmas, and all through the store,
the workers were busy, and their feet were still sore.
The tinsel was hanging. The shelves were all stocked.
Outside, it's snowing, and the store doors were locked.
The bosses bark orders. They check all their shelves.
There's an underweight Santa with two ugly elves.
Outside, a crowd's forming—no smiles on their faces.
Dad's circling around searching good parking places,
then—the big moment—the doors open wide.
People pushing and shoving to be first inside,
they rush down the aisles. Their kids scream and shout,
fill up the carts before the good stuff runs out.
Frenzied commotion, grabbing this, grabbing that,
some kid threw-up on Santa's red hat.
Kids open boxes. Toy dogs are barking.
Dad's still outside, searching for parking.
A mother heard yelling at her little brat,
"DON'T PICK THAT UP, JOHNNY.
NOW PUT THAT RIGHT BACK!!"
Registers ringing, the sales are fantastic.
Wallets are empty. Thank God for plastic.
Gotta get home now—it's already dark.
Dad never did find a good place to park.
A crowd's on the corner. They fidget and fuss—
Ninety-three people on a forty-foot bus.
Then, finally home, they collapse in relief.
"MERRY CHRISTMAS TO ALL
and to all a GOOD GRIEF!
Bah, Humbug.

With Bitter Hearts

Inside a church, you're to be wed.
The rings exchanged, the vows are said.
With loving hearts, you say, "I do,"
a whole new life in front of you.
It's so sad when a marriage ends
with bitter hearts.

After a while, a baby's due,
this little child, a part of you.
You are now a family
living life so happily.
It's so sad when a marriage ends
with bitter hearts.

As time goes by, it often seems
you've fallen into a dull routine.
The tension builds more every day,
not many words for you to say.
It's so sad when a marriage ends
with bitter hearts.

It seems there's always arguments.
Life's not making any sense.
There is friction constantly,
and your child's the referee.
It's so sad when a marriage ends
with bitter hearts.

You undergo a long divorce—
private lives in public courts,
false allegations, endless duration
bitterness and separation.

It's so sad when a marriage ends
with bitter hearts.

Pick up the pieces and start anew.
Your child wants no part of you.
A lesson learned, now you can see,
in this life, no guarantees.
It's so sad when a marriage ends
with bitter hearts.

On Holidays

Broken marriage, broken family, and blues.
Celebrations have new meanings for you.
Seems the memories never quite fade away.
As time goes by, tears fill my eyes on holidays.

Celebrations, decorations, and cheer—
"Merry Christmas," "Happy New Year,"
"Valentine's Day" and "Father's Day."
As time goes by, tears fill my eyes on holidays.

I remember all the things we used to do,
all the cards that were signed "I love you,"
all the gifts that were shared Christmas Day.
As time goes by, tears fill my eyes on holidays.

Easter baskets with bright, colored eggs,
"trick-or-treating," the candy we begged,
funny costumes in full masquerade.
As time goes by, tears fill my eyes on holidays.

Thanksgiving dinners that were prepared—
carve the turkey, then say a prayer.
Seems the memories never quite fade away.
As time goes by, tears fill my eyes on holidays.

The Crud

We were just kids in the fifties and sixties,
twelve or thirteen, not into girls yet!

We were into sports, played all the sports—
regular sports like football, baseball, softball.
We played other games with different names,
games called stickball, halfball, hoseball,
paperball, wiffleball, wireball,
and a game called the crud!

That was a cruel game, the crud.
It was inspired by a girl named Maryann,
Yes, Maryann. It was a shame, the girl by that name
wasn't blessed with a beauty at all. She was plain.
Yes, it's a shame to say it all,
but she was the one who inspired the game we called
the crud!

Yes, it was cruel, this game called the crud.
The object was to touch Maryann, then touch your friend.
Say, "You got the crud," then run away.
Keep out of his reach. Avoid him all day.
He has to touch you or some other dud.
That's the only way to get rid of the crud!
Yes, a cruel game, but we were just kids.
It was in fun, just a thing that we did.

"Wireball"—another game we played.
On our city streets, evenly spaced,
were telephone poles put into place.
When we look to the air, the wires were there.
We invented a game called wireball. We'd play with a friend with a ball,

throw the ball in the air, and hit a wire that's there.
If your aim was true, the ball would fly
and had to be caught by the other guy
on the fly!

I had a best friend, "Greenie" his name.
We all used nicknames instead of real names.
We're playing wireball—my turn to throw the ball.
It hit the wire. I had a good eye.
Greenie went running—had to catch it on the fly,
Running, full speed, that ball in his eyes,
arms outstretched, his eyes to the sky.
He just knows he's going to catch that ball.
No way he'll give me a point at all!

That's when it happened—the funniest scene—
I guess, the funniest thing I've ever seen.
Maryann was playing up the street nearby.
Greenie didn't see her with his eyes to the sky.
At full speed, he met her. They fell to the ground.
Their bodies entangled. Their arms wrapping round,
his mouth agape, his eyes opened wide—
a combination of terror and awkward surprise.
Have you ever seen Dracula when a cross is displayed?
This was the face that Greenie now made.
Maryann's eyes aflutter, a coy little smile,
Greenie climbed off her, looking defiled.
Did I laugh? Man, I laughed, laughed 'til I cried.
I laughed so hard I had pains in my side.
I said, "Man, you got the crud!" I had tears in my eyes.
"You got all of that crud for the rest of your life!"
Still laughing, I ran. I ran away—

couldn't let him touch me the rest of the day.
I know it was cruel, this kids' game we played,
but I've never laughed like I laughed that day.
As I'm writing this letter, I'm still laughing now.
As I'm thinking back, it's amazing how
this memory's lasted in such a vivid way.
a little-kid game—with me to stay!

Ballad to Bellmawr Lake

When I need a break, I know just what to do.
Take a trip to the lake. There's so much there to do.
I want to lay in the sand, the sunshine's begging me.
I want to work on that tan. That lake's the place to be.

So, why stay home doing chores?
I want to use that diving board.
When I need a break
I go to Bellmawr Lake.

There are horseshoes. There are barbecues
and smiles all around.
There are waterballs and volleyballs
with lots of picnic grounds.
There's a waterslide for the kids to ride
and music all day long,
and the golf balls I'm puttin' don't cost me nothing.
How can I go wrong?
So, when I need a break,
I go to Bellmawr Lake.

Have a day in the sun. Serve up a barbecue.
A day full of fun is what I want to do.
I get in the car. I go and spend the day.
It's not very far, just a couple of miles away,
I love the summer season.
And that lake is the reason.
So, when I need a break,
I go to Bellmawr Lake.

They are roastin' weenies, pretty girls in bikinis—
fun for one and all.

And, for the time in between, they have their own canteen—
no need to bring alcohol.
There are dancers in motion, with their suntan lotion.
Have a burger with a chocolate shake.
And, beggin' your pardon, their lifeguards are guardin',
and I know they're wide awake.
So, when I need a break, for heaven's sake,
I go to Bellmawr Lake.

Dedicated to Bob and Mary and all my friends in Bellmawr, New
Jersey